OPIUM DEN

Julie Marie Myatt

BROADWAY PLAY PUBLISHING INC
New York
www.broadwayplaypub.com
info@broadwayplaypub.com

Cover photo: Julie Marie Myatt

First edition: July 2019
I S B N: 978-0-88145-817-6

Book design: Marie Donovan
Page make-up: Adobe InDesign
Typeface: Palatino

OPIUM DEN was commissioned and developed by Yale Repertory Theatre. It was written in LosAngeles in 2012.

CHARACTERS & SETTING

MATTHEW MILTON, *photojournalist*
LIZZIE MILTON-LIGHTHOUSE, *housewife/banker's wife*
JOHN RICHARDSON, *photojournalist*
PERRY MUKAI, *photojournalist*
MAC JOHNSON, *recently retired Army sergeant/ Afghanistan veteran*
ALLEN LIGHTHOUSE, *Wall Street banker*

A video camera

A New York apartment. On the back wall, a screen will project images.

Time: The present

NOTE ON MUSIC

For performance of copyrighted songs, arrangements or recordings referenced in this play, permission of the copyright owner(s) must be obtained. Other songs, arrangements or recordings may be substituted provided permission from the copyright owner(s) of such songs, arrangements or recordings is obtained or songs, arrangements or recordings in the public domain may be substituted.

"...The rush of battle is a potent and often lethal addiction, for war is a drug, and one I ingested for many years... It can give us purpose, meaning, a reason for living. Only when we are in the midst of conflict does the shallowness and vapidness of much of our lives become apparent. Trivia dominates our conversations and increasingly our airwaves. And war is an enticing elixir. It gives us resolve, a cause. It allows us to be noble."
Chris Hedges, *War is a Force that Gives Us Meaning*

"It may strike you as strange that I who have had no pain—no acute suffering to keep down from its angles—should need opium in any shape. But I have had restlessness till it made me almost mad...as if one's life, instead of giving movement to the body, were imprisoned undiminished within it, and beating and fluttering impotently to get out, at all the doors and windows. So the medical people gave me opium—a preparation of it, called morphine, and ether—and ever since I have been calling it my amreeta...my elixir."
Elizabeth Barrett Browning, *1837*

Scene 1

(Slides: Images of American soldiers fighting the war in Afghanistan)

(A song like If It's Monday Morning *by Lee Hazlewood plays.)*

*(*LIZZIE MILTON-LIGHTHOUSE *enters and stands with her suitcase, waiting. She is wearing impeccable, expensive clothes, from head to toe. Her hair is perfect. A nice coat hangs over her arm.)*

(She looks in the distance for a car, nothing. She keeps waiting.)

(She takes a compact out of her purse, looks at herself, her lipstick, and puts it away.)

(She puts on her sunglasses.)

(Cold, she puts on her coat. Takes a scarf from her pocket.)

(She looks again for the car.)

(She puts the scarf over her hair.)

(Stares straight ahead)

(Checks her watch)

(Adjusts her scarf)

(Looks for the car again)

(Finally, she sees the car O S, tries to smile, picks up her suitcase, and exits towards it.)

Scene 2

(The song continues, the images fade, and lights up on a dirty New York apartment. [It looks as if someone left the place in a hurry, over and over again.] Old and new camera equipment is strewn about. Clothes. Unpacked boxes. A bed. A tattered couch. A few chairs. A couple of the same Afghanistan war photos from earlier are tacked up with thumb tacks on the walls. Photos of other far flung war zones, poverty, and faces of tragedy. A few photography awards lean against the wall, [half showing them off—half trying to look like he's not showing them off.])

(MATTHEW MILTON and LIZZIE enter the room. He carries her suitcase. He is dressed in roughed-up jeans and t-shirt, leather coat.)

(She keeps her coat on.)

MATTHEW: I guess we can just put your stuff down anywhere. He sets down the suitcase. Make yourself at home.

(LIZZIE tries to smile.)

LIZZIE: Thank you.
(Silence)
I like what you've done with the place. The decor.

MATTHEW: Yeah. Well.

(LIZZIE and MATTHEW both look at the place together.)

MATTHEW: I'm not here much.

LIZZIE: I can stay at a hotel.

MATTHEW: No.

LIZZIE: I'd really rather.

MATTHEW: No no.
(Silence)
This will be good.

*(He checks his cell phone. Puts it in his pocket. Distracted.
To himself)*
Okay.

LIZZIE: Okay what?

MATTHEW: Nothing. Sorry. Let's see… Well. *(He looks
around.)*

(LIZZIE looks around.)

MATTHEW: What should we do? You want a cup of tea
or something?
(He walks to the kitchen area.)

LIZZIE: Do you have rats?

MATTHEW: No.

LIZZIE: I will scream bloody murder if I see one.
Seriously. Did you know I almost got bit once?

MATTHEW: No.

LIZZIE: I did. Last year. It was awful.

(MATTHEW looks around the kitchen.)

MATTHEW: Glad to hear you survived.

LIZZIE: Barely.
(She fixes her hair.)
It was him or me.
(She pulls her coat around herself.)

(MATTHEW combs through a bare cupboard.)

LIZZIE: Why do you keep this place?

MATTHEW: I need someplace to come home to.

LIZZIE: Get married.

MATTHEW: You want milk or sugar?

LIZZIE: Milk if you have it. A woman would never live
like this.

MATTHEW: Sorry. I don't have milk.

LIZZIE: Sugar then.

(After tearing through the cabinet. Finally)

MATTHEW: I don't have tea.

(He finds a box of crackers.)

Cracker?

LIZZIE: No.

(MATTHEW tastes the cracker, quickly spits it out.)

MATTHEW: (Jesus.)

(He looks at the date on the box. And grabs a dish towel to wipe his tongue.)

(LIZZIE watches MATTHEW do this.)

MATTHEW: I'll, I'll go to the store.

LIZZIE: Don't go for me.

MATTHEW: We have to have food.

(Silence)

(MATTHEW looks through the bare cupboard. Checks other boxes and tosses them in the trash)

LIZZIE: I'm sorry you had to do this.

MATTHEW: Do what?

LIZZIE: Come home.

MATTHEW: It's not a problem.

LIZZIE: I don't believe that.

MATTHEW: It was time anyway.

LIZZIE: Why?

MATTHEW: Let's make a grocery list. What do you want?

(He grabs a small note pad from his pocket.)

LIZZIE: Were you supposed to come home?

MATTHEW: No.

LIZZIE: So why was it time?

MATTHEW: It just was. I have things to take care of.
Coffee?

LIZZIE: Yes. What kind of things?

MATTHEW: They let you have caffeine?

(LIZZIE just looks at MATTHEW.)

LIZZIE: "They"?

MATTHEW: It's a reasonable question.

LIZZIE: Of course "they" do.

MATTHEW: Well—

LIZZIE: I can have caffeine. Sugar. And cigarettes.

MATTHEW: You smoke?

LIZZIE: No, but I'm thinking of starting.
(Silence)
I have to have some pleasure.

(MATTHEW starts to write things down.)

MATTHEW: Coffee.

LIZZIE: I won't let them take away everything.

MATTHEW: You take cream in your coffee?

LIZZIE: I'm a human being for Christ's sake. Some
pleasure is important.

MATTHEW: As a human being, do you take cream in
your coffee?

LIZZIE: Yes.

MATTHEW: What else do you like?

LIZZIE: I don't care. Buy what you like.

MATTHEW: I like anything. I'm sure you eat healthy.

LIZZIE: Used to.

MATTHEW: So what to do you eat now?

LIZZIE: I'm not that interested in food.

MATTHEW: I see that. You look terrible.

LIZZIE: I haven't been down to this weight since I was sixteen.

MATTHEW: But you're not sixteen.
(Silence)
I'll go to the health food store.

LIZZIE: Do what you want. I don't care.

MATTHEW: *(He keeps writing.)* Don't start.

LIZZIE: I can go to a hotel. I won't disturb you with my "terrible" looking self.

MATTHEW: Okay.

LIZZIE: You don't look all that great yourself, by the way, but I was kind enough to keep my opinions to myself—

MATTHEW: You're staying here.

LIZZIE: There's only one bed.

MATTHEW: You'll sleep in the bed and I'll sleep on the couch.

LIZZIE: That's horrible for your back.

MATTHEW: I've been sleeping on a cot for a year—

LIZZIE: And there's no privacy. We need our privacy. And there's no television. What are we going to do all day? It's a bad arrangement already, Matthew. When was the last time you cleaned this place?

MATTHEW: It's fine.

LIZZIE: I want to call Allen.

MATTHEW: Why?

LIZZIE: This is ridiculous.

MATTHEW: Okay—

LIZZIE: He's not "ready" to see me? Sarah's not "ready" to see me? I've been gone two months! Give me a homecoming party, for Christ's sake! Pick me up, kiss me and tell me you love me and everything's going to be alright!

MATTHEW: Okay, Lizzie—

LIZZIE: But no. He's not done punishing me. So he calls you, makes a deal. "Pick her up. Take her home. Don't let her out of your sight." It's a very Allen move. Make her stay with her brother. More contol. More shame. It's never enough for him.
(Silence)
It's my house. I should be able to go home.

MATTHEW: Still. Why don't you wait a bit.

LIZZIE: Why?

MATTHEW: Wait a few days. Play his game. Settle in before you try and talk to him.

LIZZIE: I don't want to settle in. This is a shit hole.

MATTHEW: It is not.

LIZZIE: It is. I should be able to go home. It's my house too.

MATTHEW: I thought you hated that house.
(Silence)

LIZZIE: It's the principle.
(Silence)
Treating me like an outcast. Making rules.

MATTHEW: Put the phone away. Sit down. Forget Allen. Forget the house. Relax. Enjoy your time with me.
(He smiles.)
(LIZZIE smiles back.)

LIZZIE: Matthew.

MATTHEW: Yes?

LIZZIE: Are you going to do this the whole time?

MATTHEW: What?

LIZZIE: Boss me. Patronize me. Smile.

MATTHEW: I'm not bossing you—

LIZZIE: I don't need you adding more rules on my life. All I have are rules and restrictions and "no'" and "don'ts" and "not yets" and "we'll see"—

MATTHEW: I really don't have the patience for your shit right now, Lizzie. I'm tired. It took me two days to get home. Do you like cheese? What kind? Cheddar? Swiss? I can get both—

LIZZIE: Then don't boss me.

(MATTHEW sighs.)

LIZZIE: I hate this place.
(She adjusts her shirt.)
I need a flea collar.

MATTHEW: *(He keeps writing.)* I'm sure you've seen worse. Cheese?

LIZZIE: Brie. You don't know what I've seen.
(She takes some hand sanitizer out of her purse and puts it on.)

MATTHEW: And I don't want to know. Believe me. You eat meat?

LIZZIE: No.

MATTHEW: Eggs?

LIZZIE: I'm tired of everyone telling me what to do. I'm not a fucking child.

MATTHEW: Eggs?

LIZZIE: No.

MATTHEW: You got yourself into this mess. Chicken?

(LIZZIE *kicks the note pad out of* MATTHEW's *hands.*)

LIZZIE: I know exactly what I did. I have seen worse, but those places weren't my brother's home. And, the people who lived there, didn't treat me like a child. They were very kind to me.

MATTHEW: Of course they were.

LIZZIE: If you plan on spending every minute shoving this in my face, just because you can, because now *I'm* the fuck-up in the family, don't do me any favors. I'll stay in a hotel until Allen finishes rubbing my nose in my shit—

MATTHEW: I've never been the fuck-up in the family. Mom and Dad were both always very proud and supportive—

LIZZIE: Good for you—

MATTHEW: And if you think this makes me happy, that smack has done more to your brain than being married to that asshole.

LIZZIE: Then why are you helping him?

MATTHEW: I love you and I want you to be able to see your daughter again.

LIZZIE: You barely know who she is.

MATTHEW: She needs a mother. And you need to get your shit together and be there for her. We both know how important that is.
(*He picks up the note pad.*)
Now was that a yes or no on the chicken?

(LIZZIE *sits down and opens her purse and puts on her lipstick.*)

(*She takes out her cell phone.*)

MATTHEW: Who are you calling?

LIZZIE: Fuck the chicken.

MATTHEW: Lizzie?

LIZZIE: Do I have to ask your permission to talk to my friends?

MATTHEW: Is it one of your new friends?

LIZZIE: "New"?
(She stops dialing.)
Just how stupid do you think I am?

MATTHEW: You want me to answer that?

LIZZIE: Okay Matthew. Go ahead.
(She puts away the phone.)
I could feel it in the car, mile after mile, just eating through the silence. Let me have it. Belittle me, shame me—

(JOHN RICHARDSON enters, smiling.)

JOHN: I thought I heard you walking around down here.

MATTHEW: Yep. Just got in.

JOHN: Welcome home, man. Long time no see. Wow.

(JOHN walks over and hugs MATTHEW.)

MATTHEW: Yeah. Thanks thanks.

JOHN: You lost weight.

(MATTHEW looks at himself.)

MATTHEW: I hadn't really noticed—

JOHN: How was it? Get some good stuff?

MATTHEW: Good. Good. Yeah, I think I got some great stuff that—

JOHN: *(To LIZZIE)* Sorry. I don't think we've met.

LIZZIE: No.

MATTHEW: This is my sister. Lizzie.

LIZZIE: Elizabeth. Please.

MATTHEW: Elizabeth?

LIZZIE: I prefer Elizabeth. Now.

JOHN: Elizabeth.

LIZZIE: Nice to meet you.

(JOHN *shakes* LIZZIE*'s hand. Very firmly and vigorously)*

JOHN: Wow.

LIZZIE: Not used to seeing women in here?

JOHN: No. No. There's usually plenty. But never Matthew's sister.

LIZZIE: *(To* MATTHEW*)* Plenty.

JOHN: You live in the city?

LIZZIE: Gosh no. No. Connecticut.

JOHN: Nice.

LIZZIE: It can be.

JOHN: Just here for a visit?

LIZZIE: Briefly. Yes.

JOHN: I see. Well. Welcome.
(To MATTHEW*)*
I didn't know you had a sister.

MATTHEW: I do.

JOHN: And she lives so close.

LIZZIE: Technically. But he's never here, so… We aren't close. Really.

JOHN: You have any more siblings?

MATTHEW: No.

LIZZIE: He's the oldest.

JOHN: *(To* MATTHEW*)* I have four. Did you know that?

MATTHEW: I think so.

JOHN: I'm the youngest.

MATTHEW: Right, right.

JOHN: I don't see them much. They all live in Florida.

MATTHEW: Uh huh.

JOHN: Yep.
(Silence)
That's my story.
(Silence)
And I'm sticking to it.
(He smiles at LIZZIE.*)*
You guys don't look alike.

LIZZIE: We're both adopted.

JOHN: Really? Wow.

LIZZIE: Uh huh.

JOHN: *(To* MATTHEW*)* You never told me that.

*(*MATTHEW *checks his phone. Then puts it away)*

MATTHEW: Now you know.

LIZZIE: How do you know Matthew? Just neighbors
or—

JOHN: We've worked together. Many times. Many
times.

LIZZIE: Are you a photographer too—

JOHN: I am.

MATTHEW: He's good.

JOHN: I am.

LIZZIE: You work for the Times too?

JOHN: Reuters.

MATTHEW: How was Somalia?

JOHN: Fine.

MATTHEW: You get some good stuff?

JOHN: Yeah. Yeah. Amazing, actually.

MATTHEW: You look pretty thin yourself.

JOHN: Yeah, well. Somalia. Not there for the food.

MATTHEW: Can I see what you got?

JOHN: Sure. Sure. I guess so.

LIZZIE: I don't know how you guys do what you do. Risking your life for a photo. I'm not sure it's worth it.

MATTHEW: It's our job.

LIZZIE: But whose looking at your photos? Really? Who reads the paper anymore? Who watches your documentaries? It's all too depressing.

MATTHEW: Okay.

LIZZIE: Look at that…oh, what's her name…the photographer who shoots all the cute tiny babies… shit, what's her name? …She dresses them like flowers…and hides them in eggs and…oh, they are so adorable…you know who I'm talking about.

(Silence)

JOHN: Anne Geddes.

LIZZIE: Yes. Thank you. See, Anne Geddes knows her audience. She knows people want to look at cute, adorable, sleeping babies. People love her stuff. Who are your photos for?

MATTHEW: Lizzie—

LIZZIE: I think you should ask yourself.

MATTHEW: Okay—

LIZZIE: Everyone has a cell phone with a camera. Everyone's a photographer. Instagram. Twitter. Facebook. Everyone's posting images. Usually faster than you guys can do it. Photojournalists are a dying breed. Don't you think?

(Long silence)

JOHN: What do you do?

MATTHEW: She's a housewife.

LIZZIE: In a nut shell. Yes. Thank you, Matthew.

JOHN: Really? My mother was a housewife.

LIZZIE: Interesting.

JOHN: Yeah.
(Silence)
She went crazy. Our house was a mess and kind of a war zone growing up. My dad was a tyrant, and a drunk, so I guess I can't blame it all on her.

LIZZIE: No.

JOHN: I mean, I used to. Believe me. She's on drugs now. Lots of drugs. They help.

LIZZIE: Really?

JOHN: The drugs take away most of the crazy. I think she had other plans for her life. Other dreams. Something. I don't know… But, she is my mother. I love her.

MATTHEW: John—

JOHN: I don't understand her of course, but I love her. I can't help it, I guess. Loving her. She's my mother. I have to. But, she's crazy. That's for sure.
(To MATTHEW)
Did I ever tell you about her?

MATTHEW: Yes.

JOHN: She lives in Florida. In a nursing home.

MATTHEW: I think I remember that.

JOHN: It's for the best. Really.

(Silence)
That's my story.
(He smiles.)
I'm sticking to it.
(Silence)
I was, was just thinking she was a housewife too. It's probably a harder job than most people think.
(Silence)
What's your husband do?

LIZZIE: Are you married, John?

JOHN: No.

LIZZIE: Girlfriend?

JOHN: It's an on and off kind of thing. Off right now, but—

LIZZIE: And Matthew isn't married. Of course.

JOHN: Unless he's got some Afghani bride somewhere. Right, Matthew? Ship in every port?

(MATTHEW stares at JOHN.)

LIZZIE: So neither of you has a *wife*, nor has been a wife.

JOHN: Nope.

LIZZIE: And you know nothing *really* about being a wife or *house*wife. Or what it might entail. Or cost. Or feel like.

(Silence)

JOHN: True.

LIZZIE: So let's just leave it at that. You're full of shit. I'm full of shit. We're all full of shit. We know nothing about each other's lives or professions or unlived dreams. We don't care that much. We're too busy. Right Matthew?

MATTHEW: No.

LIZZIE: It's all projection and guessing and judgement. We're ignorant really, and most of the time, we would rather stay that way.

MATTHEW: Is that what your therapist says?

JOHN: I like you.

LIZZIE: Thank you.

JOHN: You're smart. I can tell.

LIZZIE: I need to be liked right now.
(She smiles at JOHN.)
And "smart". Oh John. Aren't you an angel. Turn around and let me look for your wings.

MATTHEW: Give me a fucking break.

LIZZIE: Well it's true. Who likes me? You? Allen? Sarah?

MATTHEW: Uh huh.

LIZZIE: And everyone thinks I'm stupid. Except for John here. Telling me just what I need to hear. Like a dawn of hope.

JOHN: That's me. A dawn of hope.

LIZZIE: He's my only friend.

MATTHEW: Okay. John, do you mind—

(JOHN checks his watch. Claps his hands)

JOHN: Happy hour. You guys want a drink?

MATTHEW: Smells like you've already started.

JOHN: That was just a beer with lunch.

LIZZIE: What do you have?

JOHN: I have beer, of course, wine, some vodka, scotch, bourbon, maybe some gin, I'd have to look for that—

MATTHEW: She can't. John, we're kind of in the middle of something—

JOHN: What? Too early?
(He checks his watch again.)
Nope. I don't think so.

LIZZIE: *Technically*, I just got out of rehab.

JOHN: Yikes. And here I am asking you to have a drink.
Ah, man…I'm sorry. Wow. Stupid me—

LIZZIE: Not for drinking.

JOHN: Oh—

LIZZIE: Heroin. But they took away everything. For the
moment. So… Here I am. Stranded. With my brother as
my warden.

MATTHEW: Did you really have to tell him?

LIZZIE: What?

MATTHEW: So proudly?

LIZZIE: What do you want me to do, whisper it?

MATTHEW: Yes. Please. Keep it to yourself.

LIZZIE: I'm an honest person. I like heroin. A lot. These
things happen.

MATTHEW: Uh huh.

LIZZIE: And now I'm in recovery. What? You want me
to hide in the closet and sit in a puddle of guilt?

MATTHEW: It's not a terrible idea.

JOHN: Heroin?

LIZZIE: Yes.

JOHN: Really?

LIZZIE: Yes.

JOHN: I can't believe it.

LIZZIE: Believe it.

(JOHN smiles at LIZZIE. Taking her in)

JOHN: I misjudged you.

LIZZIE: Most people do.

JOHN: You shoot up or smoke it…what?

MATTHEW: Alright—

LIZZIE: Both. I wasn't picky.

MATTHEW: John—

JOHN: What?

MATTHEW: This isn't the time. Please leave.

JOHN: I'm sorry. I'm just interested.

LIZZIE: Thank you. I appreciate your interest. See, now that's making an effort, Matthew. To understand. To know.

JOHN: Your family has a destructive streak.

LIZZIE: Apparently.
(She smiles. Shrugs)
We must want to kill ourselves. Maybe it's a seventh sense. Death. Right Matthew?

MATTHEW: Speak for yourself.

LIZZIE: Do you think it came from both our mothers? Rejecting us at birth? Or maybe their desire to kill us? Or us just not feeling—

MATTHEW: Stop it.

LIZZIE: I'd really never thought of it that way until just now.

JOHN: Why do you want to kill yourself?
(He sits down next to her.)

MATTHEW: You're drunk, John. Go home.

JOHN: I'm not drunk.
(To LIZZIE)
My mother tried to kill herself. Twice.

LIZZIE: Really?

JOHN: Yes. It was awful. Go ahead.
(*He crosses his legs, getting comfortable.*)

LIZZIE: Personally, I don't think I want to die. Per say.
Not consciously. It's all unconscious, of course. (This
is what I learned in therapy. I found it fascinating.) I
don't want death as a state of being…the end, good-
bye…I just want to get close to it.

JOHN: Huh.

LIZZIE: Touch it. Kiss it's lips.

JOHN: Uh huh.

LIZZIE: Feel the cold bright breath of the other side.
Like a new lover. And yet, stay. Stay here, in life.

MATTHEW: (Jesus Christ)

JOHN: How did it start?

MATTHEW: John.

JOHN: The heroin.

LIZZIE: How much time do you have?

JOHN: Was it through a friend? A lover?

LIZZIE: Yes. And yes.

MATTHEW: Now isn't the time to talk about this.

JOHN: Am I making you uncomfortable?

LIZZIE: No.

MATTHEW: She just got out today, John. This isn't good
for her recovery.

LIZZIE: Says who?

JOHN: How long were you there?

LIZZIE: Two months.

JOHN: How was your stay?

LIZZIE: I learned a lot about myself.

JOHN: Of course.

LIZZIE: Though now I find myself wondering if self-knowledge is ultimately just another black hole.

JOHN: Really? How so?

LIZZIE: I'm a mess.

JOHN: Isn't everyone?

LIZZIE: Yes.

MATTHEW: Stop, John—

JOHN: Is this a sensitive subject?

LIZZIE: No. Not really.

MATTHEW: She's not a story.

JOHN: I didn't say she was—

MATTHEW: Back off, man. Okay? Go home.

JOHN: What? I'm curious. I can't be curious?

MATTHEW: Why?

JOHN: It seems unusual, for someone of her, of her.... obvious education and, and income level.
(To LIZZIE*)*
You're very wealthy?

LIZZIE: Yes.

JOHN: Is heroin a problem in Connecticut?

LIZZIE: No.

MATTHEW: John.

LIZZIE: Unless you're looking for it.

JOHN: Were you looking for it?

LIZZIE: Apparently.

JOHN: Why?

MATTHEW: You see what he's doing?

LIZZIE: He's asking me questions, which is a hell of a lot more than you've done in the past year.

JOHN: Why were you looking for it?

LIZZIE: I didn't know that I was looking for it, in the beginning.

JOHN: Really? So then how—

MATTHEW: Stop. Go home.

JOHN: *(To* MATTHEW*)* I'm having a conversation here.

LIZZIE: Have you ever tried it, John?

JOHN: No.

LIZZIE: Have you ever been desperate to escape yourself?

JOHN: Uh. No. I don't know. Maybe. Sure. Probably. No. I don't know—

LIZZIE: Well. Then maybe you don't know why I'd look for it.

MATTHEW: Lizzie—

LIZZIE: And…it's wonderful. I mean… Heaven. Absolute heaven. Beyond…B etter than any orgasm. Seriously.
(She winks.)
At least the kind I used to have with my husband. So, you know.

JOHN: Do you mind if I get my camera? I'd love to record this.

MATTHEW: I knew it. Fuck you. Get out.

LIZZIE: Record what?

JOHN: You. Talking.

LIZZIE: About?

JOHN: Your experience with heroin. Nothing fancy. Just you talking.

LIZZIE: Sure. Why not. Sounds fun.

MATTHEW: No—

LIZZIE: Though Matthew says I look terrible. I had to use some cheap Clairol hair dye—

MATTHEW: Absolutely not, Lizzie. No—

LIZZIE: *Elizabeth.* I've got nothing else to do. You want to talk to me about this?
(Silence)
I didn't think so.

JOHN: I'm fascinated by addiction. How it starts.
(To MATTHEW*)*
Remember that piece I did on meth in—

MATTHEW: No.

LIZZIE: You don't think my life is interesting enough, Matthew?

MATTHEW: I don't think it needs to be documented. Right now. Like this.

LIZZIE: Why not?

MATTHEW: It's your personal life. Your very personal life.

LIZZIE: To you or me?

MATTHEW: Both.

LIZZIE: Well, that's your problem, not mine.

MATTHEW: You are barely clean.

LIZZIE: And I could use a distraction. Talking about it is good for me—

MATTHEW: John, man, I'm asking you to please stay away from this.

JOHN: Seems like it's Elizabeth's choice.

MATTHEW: But I'm asking you to leave her alone.

JOHN: Seems it's Elizabeth's say, not yours.

LIZZIE: Thank you.

MATTHEW: As my friend...please, don't. Don't.

JOHN: As your friend?

MATTHEW: Yes.

JOHN: Your *friend*?

MATTHEW: Yes.

JOHN: Remember the time we hit the I E D in Iraq and that corporal was—

MATTHEW: You're bringing that up? Now? Really?

JOHN: And—

MATTHEW: That was different—

JOHN: I said, I said, "don't shoot that, Matt. Please don't. That's not human anymore. There's got to be a limit. I don't want to remember this. Please put the camera down—"

MATTHEW: You're still harboring resentment from/ that—

JOHN: And you shot it anyway.

MATTHEW: That was seven years ago.

JOHN: So—

MATTHEW: I was on assignment. It was my job. And yours.

JOHN: You took the pictures and made sure they were submitted for every prize in the country. Every single fucking prize—

MATTHEW: If you hadn't been so fucking afraid to crawl for your camera, you would have done the same.

JOHN: No—

MATTHEW: You just didn't want me to get what you couldn't.

JOHN: There's got to be some, some dignity.

MATTHEW: For what?

JOHN: That was a man's life.

MATTHEW: And I showed that. I showed that.

JOHN: His face was gone.

MATTHEW: That was the point! That is my job.

JOHN: There's got to be a limit.

MATTHEW: Yeah? She's my sister. This is my home. My life. Here's *my* limit.

JOHN: She's a living, *conscious* being making a choice to have her life documented. She has a fucking *face*.

LIZZIE: It's a little tired, but yes.

MATTHEW: *Now* you're changing the rules because you lost one chance seven fucking years ago to take a picture that I won an award for—

JOHN: Two awards.
(Pointing against the wall)
They're right over there—

MATTHEW: So—

JOHN: There's got to be some dignity.

MATTHEW: What does that even mean?

JOHN: I don't know anymore.

MATTHEW: Because it's just some bullshit excuse—

LIZZIE: Well, as much as I'd love to talk war stories with you boys, I've got to use the ladies room. Where is it, please?

MATTHEW: Over there. The door doesn't really close, so use your foot.

LIZZIE: My foot?

MATTHEW: Just...

(MATTHEW shows LIZZIE.)

LIZZIE: How do you live like this? Talk about dignity.
(She stands up.)
I better not see a rat.
(She straightens her clothes.)
If John thinks I'm interesting and wants to record me talking about myself, let him. I'm flattered. Let me be flattered.

MATTHEW: You don't understand—

LIZZIE: I haven't been flattered in a long time.

MATTHEW: Jesus, Lizzie. There are other ways to be fucking flattered—

LIZZIE: It might be good for me. I might learn something more about myself. My therapist thinks its good for me to express myself and—

MATTHEW: And when he sells it? What will you learn?

JOHN: Whose talking selling it?

MATTHEW: You didn't have to.

JOHN: I'm not going to sell it. I'm just interested.

MATTHEW: Why?

LIZZIE: So what if he sells it. Maybe I'll be famous. Help people. Change lives. Save the world.

MATTHEW: Uh huh.

LIZZIE: You just don't want me to be famous.

MATTHEW: For ruining your daughter's life? For embarrassing your family? For being found naked and drooling with a needle in your arm? No.

(Silence)

Talk about dignity.

(Silence)

Thank god Mom and Dad aren't alive.

LIZZIE: I see.

(Silence)

I see.

(Silence)

John, please go get your camera. And the wine. If you would like to drink it. None for me, thank you. I'll touch up my face. And see what I can do with this hair.

MATTHEW: Lizzie—

(LIZZIE exits.)

(JOHN stands up.)

MATTHEW: You're an asshole. Fuck you.

JOHN: You're overreacting.

MATTHEW: Do you realize how hard it was to come home for this?

JOHN: You heard what she said. It could be good for her. And I need something light, something domestic, to clear my head of Somalia.

MATTHEW: This isn't light!

JOHN: You know what I mean—

MATTHEW: I don't care about you. What about what she needs?

JOHN: Can't she decide that for herself?

MATTHEW: She's an addict. And so are you, by the way.

JOHN: I think you're underestimating her—I had two, maybe three beers, big deal—

MATTHEW: You spend five minutes with my sister and think you know anything about—

JOHN: No, but I'm willing to sit and listen.

MATTHEW: Just out of the goodness of your heart.

JOHN: Yes.

MATTHEW: Do it without the camera.
(Silence)
She's my sister and she's in trouble. This part of her life doesn't need to be documented.

JOHN: This could be a very interesting project—I need a—

MATTHEW: I don't care.

JOHN: This could help both of us.

MATTHEW: I don't care. Leave my sister alone.

JOHN: But—

MATTHEW: I mean it. Please. Don't.

(LIZZIE returns.)

LIZZIE: Well. That was an experience. I feel like I'm camping.
(To JOHN)
Where's your camera? Go get it.

(Silence)

JOHN: Maybe, maybe we can start tomorrow. I need to catch up on some work, and you should probably get some rest anyway. Right?

LIZZIE: What did you say to him?

MATTHEW: Nothing—

LIZZIE: Is everyone my parent now?

JOHN: No—

LIZZIE: I'll decide when I want to rest or eat or talk or call or sing or shit or love or whatever the hell I want to do.

I made one mistake.

MATTHEW: One?

LIZZIE: And I just spent two months paying for it. So let me enjoy myself. Dammit, Matthew! Let me live! It's not that much to ask! Let me live a little!

MATTHEW: You've been living plenty.

LIZZIE: Fuck you.

(*Silence*)

JOHN: I'll, I'll come by tomorrow morning.

LIZZIE: Bring your camera.

JOHN: Have a good night.
(*He looks at* MATTHEW *and exits.*)

LIZZIE: Are you afraid I'm going to say something about you? I'm going to tarnish your reputation?

MATTHEW: No.

LIZZIE: I appreciate you flying home, and participating in Allen's "deal" to pick me up and take me in, but that doesn't mean you get to dictate my life the way he does.

MATTHEW: I'm not trying to.

LIZZIE: I'll walk out right now. And neither of you will see me again.

MATTHEW: Really?

LIZZIE: I'll just disappear.

MATTHEW: And then what?

(*Silence*)

LIZZIE: I need a reason to get up in the morning.

MATTHEW: You have a family.

LIZZIE: Where are they?
(*She looks around.*)

I need something to do, Matthew. I can't just sit here all day. Waiting to go home. He thinks I'm interesting.

MATTHEW: You are.

LIZZIE: He can sit and ask me all the questions and hear all the answers you don't want to know.

MATTHEW: That's not true.

LIZZIE: Well, it doesn't matter anyway. This is my choice, not yours. I don't need your permission.

(Silence)

MATTHEW: Let me see your phone for a minute.

LIZZIE: Why?

MATTHEW: Just let me see it.

LIZZIE: Why?

MATTHEW: Just…

(LIZZIE hands it to MATTHEW. He puts it in his pocket.)

LIZZIE: Hey.

(MATTHEW picks up his coat.)

LIZZIE: Where are you going?

MATTHEW: Outside. I've got to make a phone call.

LIZZIE: To who? Allen?

MATTHEW: No.

LIZZIE: With my phone?

MATTHEW: No.

LIZZIE: Then give it back.

MATTHEW: No.

LIZZIE: Give it back.

MATTHEW: No.

LIZZIE: You don't trust me?

MATTHEW: Do whatever the hell you want with John, Lizzie.

LIZZIE: Elizabeth—

MATTHEW: I don't care. Talk your heart out. But don't blame me when it comes back and bites you in the ass.

LIZZIE: Why would I blame you?

(MATTHEW *opens the door.*)

LIZZIE: Who are you calling?

(MATTHEW *exits.*)

(LIZZIE *looks around the apartment.*)

Scene 3

(*Slide: A soldier's face, screaming.*)

(*Night*)

LIZZIE: Matthew?
(*Silence*)
Matthew?

MATTHEW: Hmm.

LIZZIE: I didn't hear you come in.
(*Silence*)
A long call?

MATTHEW: Yes.

LIZZIE: Who was it?

MATTHEW: No one you know.
(*Silence*)

LIZZIE: Can we turn on a light?

MATTHEW: Why?

LIZZIE: It's too dark in here.
(*Silence*)

Where are the street lights? Are those black-out
curtains?

(Silence)

I feel like I'm in a cave.

(Silence)

Please turn on a light.

(Silence)

I can't see myself think.

(She gets up in the dark and gropes for a light.)

(MATTHEW turns on a light.)

*(LIZZIE's wearing a nice silk nightgown. She steps on
something.)*

LIZZIE: Has this floor *ever* been vacuumed?

MATTHEW: I don't know.

LIZZIE: Do you own a vacumm?

MATTHEW: No.

LIZZIE: How do you live in this squalor? I know you
make some money. There's no reason to live this way.

(MATTHEW lies back down.)

LIZZIE: You're too old.

(Silence)

It really does look like a junkie house, Matthew. I'm
not kidding.

(She laughs.)

MATTHEW: Then you must feel at home.

LIZZIE: I guess you think I deserve that.

(Silence)

I'm sorry I disappointed you. But I'm not sorry for
what I did. It may have been foolish, but it's something
I had to do.

MATTHEW: Had to?

LIZZIE: I have felt more alive in the past year than I've ever felt.

(*Silence*)

How fucked up is that?

MATTHEW: I don't know.

LIZZIE: What am I going to do now?

MATTHEW: Go to sleep.

LIZZIE: Matthew?

MATTHEW: I'll leave the light on.

LIZZIE: Seriously. How am I going to be normal again? I don't want to be normal.

MATTHEW: I hate to tell you this, but you've never really been "normal". I don't know where you got that.

LIZZIE: Matthew.

MATTHEW: I mean it. You're probably one of the weirdest people I know.

(*Silence*)

LIZZIE: You're just saying that to cheer me up.

MATTHEW: I'm not.

LIZZIE: Yes you are.

(*Silence*)

How weird do you think I am?

(MATTHEW *sighs.*)

LIZZIE: Really.

MATTHEW: I'm tired and jet-lagged—

LIZZIE: Just tell me. On a scale from one to ten, one being slightly weird, ten being extremely weird, where do I sit?

(MATTHEW *sighs again.*)

LIZZIE: When did you start sighing so much? You sound like an old man. Afghanistan is aging you. Is it really worth it?

MATTHEW: Eight.

LIZZIE: Eight what?

MATTHEW: Eight. Weird.

LIZZIE: Really?

MATTHEW: Pretty much.

LIZZIE: Really?

MATTHEW: Yes.

LIZZIE: Why?

MATTHEW: Trust me.

LIZZIE: Tell me.

MATTHEW: I'm tired.

LIZZIE: If I'm an eight, I need to know why. If I was a four, you could go to bed, but an eight? Matthew. Please.

MATTHEW: I think this situation is pretty indicative of an eight.

LIZZIE: Anyone can do this.

MATTHEW: I don't think so.

LIZZIE: All you have to do is shoot some heroin, fall in love with your dealer, and you can find yourself here. Trust me.

MATTHEW: But not in your neighborhood. With your friends. Your country club. You're a trailblazer.

LIZZIE: Uh huh.

MATTHEW: You are.

(Silence)

LIZZIE: I'm a little lost.

MATTHEW: Then don't talk to John. On camera. Please.

LIZZIE: Matthew.

MATTHEW: What?

LIZZIE: It's my life.
(Silence)
I was interesting on heroin. Really interesting.
(Silence)
I miss getting high. This is very hard.
(Silence)
Is there any part of you that understands that?

MATTHEW: Yes.
(Silence)
I've got a lot to do tomorrow. Let's get some sleep.
(He reaches for the light.)

LIZZIE: Leave the light on.
(Silence)
Thanks for picking me up today.

MATTHEW: You're welcome.
(Long silence)
It's worth it.

LIZZIE: What?

MATTHEW: Afghanistan.

Scene 4

(Slide: Afghani women in a poppy field.)

(Morning)

(LIZZIE sits at the table with a small mirror to put on her make-up.)

(JOHN enters without knocking with his camera equipment, and struggles to carry two cups of coffee.)

JOHN: I brought you and Matthew coffee.

LIZZIE: He's not here.

JOHN: Oh. Where is he?

LIZZIE: Did you bring your camera?

JOHN: Yes. I did. I did. I woke up, thinking, let's do this!

LIZZIE: What did you do last night?

JOHN: Oh. Nothing much really. Hung out.

LIZZIE: You did more than that. You look awful. Drink that coffee.

JOHN: Maybe I will. But I brought it for him.

LIZZIE: I didn't sleep a wink. At one point, I didn't know where the hell I was. You ever have that when you wake up in the middle of the night and forget you're in a new place, and you look around and look around and try and figure out where you are and how you got there and you feel so...so abandoned?

JOHN: Often.

LIZZIE: It's exhausting, isn't it?

JOHN: It is.

LIZZIE: I'm sure I look a hundred. You better have some good lighting tricks.

(PERRY MUKAI *enters through the open door. He carries a tripod and a couple pots and pans.*)

PERRY: Oh. Sorry. I thought you were Matthew. I heard voices over here... Is he home?

JOHN: *(To* LIZZIE*)* This is Perry. He lives next door. *(To Perry)* Elizabeth. Matthew's sister.

PERRY: I didn't know he had a sister. Nice to meet you. You two don't look alike.

LIZZIE: Adopted.

PERRY: Really?

JOHN: What do you want, Perry?

PERRY: Just—

LIZZIE: Do you guys just wait for my brother to come home? Does he owe you guys money or something?

PERRY: No. Usually the opposite.

JOHN: What do you want?

PERRY: Just stopping by. Do you know when he'll be back?

LIZZIE: He was gone when I woke up this morning.

PERRY: I see.

LIZZIE: You a photographer too?

PERRY: Yes.

LIZZIE: How many of you live in this building?

PERRY: Nine.

LIZZIE: Nine? You can't find another building that will have you?

JOHN: Six.

PERRY: Oh. Right. Seven, actually. Two were recently killed.

LIZZIE: Really?

JOHN: How do you get seven?

PERRY: You. Me. Matthew. Rick. Todd. Ed. Alice.

JOHN: Alice shoots food.

PERRY: So what. She's good.

LIZZIE: Who does she shoot food for?

PERRY: Martha Stewart.

LIZZIE: She must be very good.

JOHN: It's food.

LIZZIE: She makes it beautiful. It never looks like that when you make it yourself. It looks like shit.

JOHN: How hard can her work be? You throw some light on the food. Take the picture.

LIZZIE: Does she have to want to get killed to take a decent photo?

JOHN: No. It's just not that hard. Trust me.

PERRY: It takes skill. A lot of skill. I've done it.

JOHN: Of course you have. You'll take any job.

PERRY: What's that supposed to mean?

LIZZIE: If it's so easy, make me look beautiful. Or do you need me to bleed, or beg or cry or explode or something?

PERRY: It helps—

JOHN: I don't think that will be a problem.

LIZZIE: I love you, John. You really are the only one who likes me right now.

JOHN: I doubt that.

(LIZZIE *puts on her lipstick.*)

LIZZIE: Well, my dog might still like me. He doesn't judge.

PERRY: Oh. What kind do you have?

LIZZIE: Dachshund.

PERRY: Wiener dog. Nice.

LIZZIE: Yes.

PERRY: They're very long—

JOHN: Don't you have someplace to be—

PERRY: And short.

(MATTHEW *enters with bags of groceries, and pushing a new vacuum.*)

MATTHEW: Hi.

PERRY: Hey, man.

MATTHEW: How's it going?

PERRY: Good. Good. Working hard. Welcome back. Nice vacuum.

MATTHEW: Did you meet my sister?

PERRY: I did. I didn't know you had a sister—

MATTHEW: And I see John is ready for business. Ready to work.

JOHN: We've decided, we're going to go ahead do this little project. Nothing fancy. See what happens.

PERRY: What are you doing?

JOHN: Nothing.

MATTHEW: Did you sign a release form, Lizzie?

JOHN: Not yet.

LIZZIE: We don't want to be in your way.

JOHN: We could go upstairs.

MATTHEW: She stays here.

PERRY: What are you—

LIZZIE: You're going to have to let me out of here sometime.

MATTHEW: I will. But not to John's place.

LIZZIE: Why not?

PERRY: What are you working on?

JOHN: None of your business.

PERRY: Is it a story—

JOHN: I said, none of your business.

(MATTHEW *begins to put away the groceries.*)

(LIZZIE *continues to put on her make-up.*)

PERRY: I borrowed these while you were gone.

(PERRY *hands the tripod to* MATTHEW.)

MATTHEW: Okay.

PERRY: And these. Thanks.

(PERRY *hands* MATTHEW *the pots and pans.*)

PERRY: I'd love to see what you got. You see plenty of action over there?

MATTHEW: Yes. But this is not a good time.

JOHN: What do you want, Perry?

PERRY: I'll just, just come by later.

MATTHEW: Thanks. Good to see you. We'll catch up then.

PERRY: Got it. I understand. Great. Great. Maybe I can borrow that vacuum sometime?

MATTHEW: Yeah.

PERRY: *(To* LIZZIE*)* Nice to meet you, Elizabeth.
(*He exits.*)

(JOHN *watches the door close.*)

(MATTHEW *continues to put away the groceries.*)

(JOHN *looks at* MATTHEW.)

JOHN: I brought you some coffee. But I, I, uh, started to drink it, so…
(*Silence*)
You can still have it if you want. I didn't drink that much.

(MATTHEW *ignores* JOHN.)

JOHN: I'll finish it. I guess I'll just finish it myself. What the hell.

(He drinks the coffee. Burning his lip)

*(*MATTHEW *checks his phone.)*

LIZZIE: Matthew?

(Silence)

Matthew?

MATTHEW: What?

LIZZIE: Where were you this morning?

MATTHEW: Why?

LIZZIE: I don't know, I just—

MATTHEW: I was shopping—

LIZZIE: You could have left a note—

MATTHEW: Sorry.

(Slide: A beautiful Afghani woman. A scarf hides everything but her eyes, staring at the camera.)

*(*LIZZIE *gets seated.)*

*(*JOHN *settles in behind the camera.)*

JOHN: Here we go.

LIZZIE: Is this okay?

JOHN: Good.

LIZZIE: How do I look?

JOHN: Beautiful.

*(*LIZZIE *smiles.)*

JOHN: So just relax and talk. Tell me how it started.

LIZZIE: Gosh. Let's see.

(She laughs.)

(I feel so nervous all the sudden.)

JOHN: Just be your charming self. You look great.

LIZZIE: Okay.

JOHN: How did it start? The heroin. Was it a bout of depression? Or—

(MATTHEW *begins to vacuum. The loud humm takes over the apartment.*)

(LIZZIE *and* JOHN *look at each other.*)

(LIZZIE *walks over an unplugs the vacuum.*)

LIZZIE: Do you have to do this now?

MATTHEW: You want it clean?

LIZZIE: Do it later.

MATTHEW: I really think I should take care of this now. You like a clean place—

(MATTHEW *walks to plug it in.* LIZZIE *stops him.*)

LIZZIE: Matthew. Please. Don't be an ass. This can wait.

(MATTHEW *pushes away the vacuum. He raises his arms in surrender, and moves to the couch, looking at his work on his computer screen, and checking his cell phone.*)

LIZZIE: John, where were we?
(*She returns to her seat.*)

(*The slide fades to the video of* LIZZIE *speaking. Occasionally* JOHN *will move the camera over to shoot* MATTHEW, *however, only when* MATTHEW *is not aware he's being filmed. The video captures* MATTHEW's *reaction to his sister story.*)

JOHN: The heroin. Was it a depression that started it?

LIZZIE: Not a depression. No. No. More just a general unhappiness.

(*Silence*)

JOHN: Can you be more specific?

LIZZIE: Well, I looked around and saw that I wasn't here nor there in my life. I was just…nothing. I was a walking body, void of purpose… With all the money

I needed, more really, and not a care in the world.
Literally, not a care. Not one. Or I thought I had no
cares….Allen and I don't, didn't talk about it much
but he was one of those guys who made a bundle on
Wall Street when that mortgage ship came in, and then
jumped off with all the money just before the big ship
sank the country. So now we are set…I mean, *set*…

JOHN: Uh huh.

LIZZIE: Of course, Allen has hidden the money in
accounts all over the world, like treasure chests…
So technically, we're pirates living in Connecticut…
Maybe some people have forgotten about us now, who
knows…but I started to see that our life, my life, was
all stolen goods…I started to see that my diamond
necklace, was someone else's house…my leather
couch and vintage Eames chairs, were someone's kids'
college fund…my daughter's private school tuition,
was someone's retirement… My Persian rugs, were the
rugs pulled out from someone else's life…so to speak.
Am, am I trying to hard? Trying to be too, I don't
know, too literary or something?

MATTHEW: Yes.

LIZZIE: I was an English major.

JOHN: No, no. You're doing great. But less hands.

LIZZIE: Okay. Well…my entire house began to look
and smell of someone else's life, lost, stolen…It began
to stink… Really stink. A horrible, horrible smell. And
I used to love my house. Really love it. I was proud of
it. I have good taste… So…it was like, like a beloved
turning on you. You know? When love suddenly
becomes repulsion. (Kind of like my daughter, but
that's another long tale of woe…and, you'd have to
talk to her about it.) Anyway, this numbness set in…
this, I don't know… Every morning, I'd make a pot of
coffee. I could hide my nose in the cup and it would

mask the smell of the house, and I'd drink the whole pot combing the internet, reading *The New York Times*, and watching youtube videos of other people's lives, other people's misfortune and then staring at the wood on my kitchen table…for hours…I mean *hours*. I would sit there and follow the pattern in the wood with my finger…I know that table very well now. It's the only furniture I have from my parents. We sold most of it when they died. Matthew and I ate breakfast at that table every day as kids. Remember that table, Matthew? …

(MATTHEW *doesn't answer.*)

LIZZIE: I'm sure you do… We did our homework there too….Matthew?

(MATTHEW *keeps working.*)

LIZZIE: I know he remembers it… He's just being difficult… Anyway…so I went to the doctor and he gave me something to help the numbness and get me away from the kitchen table and my nose out of the coffee… When that didn't do anything, he gave me something to "calm my nerves" …and then my nerves couldn't be calmed anymore with those, I asked him for something stronger to "settle my mind", and he gave me that, but my mind wasn't settled so he tried something to "lift my spirits" …and my spirits lifted for a bit, so Allen took us to the Bahamas for a vacation…I'm sorry, is this interesting? Really?

MATTHEW: No.

JOHN: Yes. Very. Keep going. Hands.

LIZZIE: Okay. When I was there, in the Bahamas, I had a panic attack in the hotel suite and didn't come out for three of our seven days there… Which probably scared my daughter to death…I feel horrible about that… (You should have seen how she looked at me.

Talk about repulsion) …Once we got back, those pills
had obviously stopped working and the doctor told
me he would see what else he could do… (He was
getting frustrated with me at this point. He was very
expensive and very highly recommended and I think
he looked at me as a failure. And, he was running out
of drugs.) So…I was in a pickle…and the crazy thing
is, Allen kept trying to buy me things to cheer me
up—more jewelry, spa days, a house in Costa Rica,
and it just made me want to sit at that kitchen table
all the more… Well, long story short, (Ha) …one day
I went out to get more coffee and met a woman at a
gas station on the way who had a look in her eye that,
she just had a look in her eye, I don't know, that had
something I wanted…I couldn't tell you what it was
exactly, but somehow I felt she knew a state of mind
I had yet to experience…she was like a magnet…I
saw my holy grail, right there…I asked her to lunch,
my treat… She took me to her friend's house and
that friend, he was the one that had what I had been
looking for all along… He gave me something that
all those pills couldn't touch… Not by a mile…And,
suddenly, I didn't care about the table anymore, the
smell, my house, the stuff, the money, anything…none
of it mattered…

MATTHEW: That's enough.

(He gets up.)

I can't take anymore of your whining. "I'm too rich.
Boo hoo." Please, Lizzie. Cry me a fucking river. Turn
it off, John.

JOHN: We're just getting started—

MATTHEW: Turn it off.

(The video goes off.)

LIZZIE: Do you remember that table?

MATTHEW: Who cares?

LIZZIE: I care. Your name is carved into a corner of it.

(Keys unlock the door.)

MATTHEW: So what.

LIZZIE: It means something to me. To see your name there. Knowing you wrote it there. Our family.

(MATTHEW hears the door and walks over as it opens. MAC JOHNSON enters wearing headphones, listening to an i-pod.)

(He takes out the head-phones.)

MAC: You scared me, man—I thought you were still in Afghanistan.

MATTHEW: Sorry. Change of plans. I had to come home.

(MAC enters carrying a small back pack.)

MATTHEW: You found the keys.

MAC: They were right where you said they'd be.

MATTHEW: I'm sorry. I completely forgot you were coming. I had to come home, quickly and—

MAC: Maybe I should go. You have company—

MATTHEW: Don't be silly. This is, this is Sergeant Johnson.

MAC: I'm not a sergeant anymore.

MATTHEW: Right. Mac. Johnson. Retired.

MAC: Yes.

MATTHEW: This is my sister, Lizzie—Elizabeth—and my neighbor John.

MAC: Are sure this is cool? Am I interrupting something?

MATTHEW: No, no. Have a seat.

MAC: I feel like I'm interrupting.

MATTHEW: No. Please. Relax.

MAC: Looks like you're filming something.

MATTHEW: And I would love for you to interrupt it.

JOHN: It, it can wait. I guess.

LIZZIE: How do you know Matthew?

MAC: Afghanistan.

LIZZIE: I see.

MAC: Maybe I should go.

MATTHEW: No, no. You're staying. Can I get you something to drink?

MAC: I wouldn't mind a beer.

MATTHEW: No booze in the house, man. Sorry.

MAC: You? No booze.

MATTHEW: Soda?

MAC: *(Laughing)* I guess. Sure. I could drink a soda.

LIZZIE: You can blame me. I just got out of rehab.

MATTHEW: Must you, Lizzie?

LIZZIE: What?

MATTHEW: Advertise? Jesus Christ.

MAC: Matthew didn't tell me he had such a foxy sister.

LIZZIE: He's ashamed of me.

MATTHEW: I am not.

LIZZIE: Then why does no one know I exist?

(MATTHEW goes to the refrigerator and gets a cola and brings it to MAC.)

(They all just stand around looking at each other.)

(JOHN shakes MAC's hand.)

JOHN: I saw the documentary Matthew made about you. Wonderful. It's nice to meet you in person. A real honor.

MAC: Thanks.

JOHN: You did some amazing things.

MAC: No.

JOHN: You did.
(Silence)
You happy to be home?

MAC: Not really.

JOHN: Right. Well. Welcome to New York. I hope to see you again.

MAC: Thanks.

JOHN: Well, I guess that's enough of me here now. Onward.
(Silence)
Elizabeth. More tomorrow?

LIZZIE: I'm all yours.

JOHN: Matthew.

(JOHN waits, MATTHEW ignores him. JOHN exits.)

(LIZZIE joins MAC on the couch.)

LIZZIE: Well. Here we are.

MAC: I didn't think anyone would be here. I feel strange—

MATTHEW: I came home to spend time with my sister.

LIZZIE: He was forced in to it.

MATTHEW: No I wasn't.

LIZZIE: By my husband.

MATTHEW: Mac was in the Army.

LIZZIE: I figured that.

MATTHEW: I did a documentary about him. When I was covering his platoon in Afghanistan two years ago. I sent it to you in March—

LIZZIE: I didn't watch it.

(*To* MAC)

Sorry. I've been busy.

MAC: Good.

LIZZIE: John is doing a documentary about me. We must be pretty interesting people.

MAC: Or suckers.

LIZZIE: You think so?

MAC: People think they know you because they saw you on T V. They don't know shit.

LIZZIE: So what's your story?

MATTHEW: (*To* LIZZIE) He was great in it. Mac's going to stay here with us.

(*To* MAC)

I'll sleep on the floor, and you can have the couch.

LIZZIE: I'll go to a hotel.

MATTHEW: No.

MAC: I don't want to put anyone out.

MATTHEW: This is fine. There's plenty of room.

MAC: No, I should go somewhere else—

MATTHEW: Where?

MAC: I don't know, but—

MATTHEW: I told you. You're welcome to stay as long as you want. It's the least I could do.

MAC: But I didn't know you all would be here—

MATTHEW: Well, neither did we. But there's plenty of room for all of us.

LIZZIE: I wouldn't call it "plenty".

MAC: Me either.

LIZZIE: I guess plenty is a matter of perspective.

MAC: I guess so.

(LIZZIE *smiles at* MAC.)

LIZZIE: But I don't mind sharing.

MAC: Me either.

(*Silence*)

MATTHEW: You can't drink or smoke pot here, Mac. Nothing. Sorry.

MAC: Oh. Okay. That's cool.

MATTHEW: I mean it. Nothing.

MAC: I heard you. I get it. No problem.

LIZZIE: And he doesn't have a television.

MAC: No T V?

LIZZIE: No.

MAC: Damn. What's wrong with you, man?

LIZZIE: I hope you like board games.

MAC: Depends on what it is.

LIZZIE: What do you have, Matthew?

MATTHEW: What?

LIZZIE: What kind of board games to you have?

(MATTHEW *just looks at* LIZZIE.)

MATTHEW: None.

LIZZIE: Of course we could play other games. Blind man's bluff. Red Rover. Freeze tag. I've got nothing but time.

MAC: I mostly know drinking games.

MATTHEW: We can sit around and talk. Catch up.

(LIZZIE *and* MAC *both look at* MATTHEW.)

LIZZIE: What brings you to New York?

MAC: No where else to go. At the moment.

(LIZZIE *holds out her hand.*)

LIZZIE: Well. That makes two of us.

(MAC *shakes* LIZZIE's *hand.*)

LIZZIE: I guess we could make a game out of that, huh? Who has the saddest story, you or me?
(*Silence*)
What's the matter?

MAC: Your hands are soft.

LIZZIE: When's the last time you touched a woman?

MAC: I just got home.

LIZZIE: I see.

MAC: I'll get around to it.

LIZZIE: So why don't you go home to your family?

MATTHEW: Mac was raised in foster care.

LIZZIE: Oh.

MATTHEW: Did you mind that I told her that? I'm sorry—

MAC: It's no secret now, is it. It's all on tape.

LIZZIE: Matthew and I were adopted. Did he tell you that?

MAC: No.

LIZZIE: He doesn't like to share his family's story. Apparently.

(MATTHEW *just looks at* LIZZIE.)

MAC: The Army was my family. But, not anymore.

LIZZIE: So what's your plan?

MATTHEW: He just got out, Lizzie.

MAC: I'm open to ideas.

LIZZIE: Ah. Okay. That will be our game, Mac. Plan
your life. I used to plan wonderful parties. Really. I'm
good at this.

(PERRY *enters holding a camera lens. And a blanket)*

PERRY: Hey.

MATTHEW: Hey.

PERRY: Is this a good time?

MATTHEW: Not really.

(PERRY *hands* MATTHEW *the lens.)*

PERRY: Oh. Well. Okay. I borrowed this while you were
gone. Thanks.
(He sees MAC.*)*
Wait. Are you Sergeant Johnson?

MAC: Mac. Please.

(PERRY *walks over and shakes* MAC's *hand.)*

PERRY: Are you here for a visit?

MAC: I am.

PERRY: It's a pleasure. Very nice to meet you, Sergeant.
I really think what you did in that fight in Kunar
Province, it, it was extremely courageous.

MAC: It was what it was.

PERRY: Very impressive. I really enjoyed Matthew's
story about you. Very compelling. Very inspiring.

MAC: Uh huh.

PERRY: So nice to meet you. I'd love to talk to you
more. If you have time.

MAC: No.

PERRY: I'm doing a series of portraits of returning
veterans, right when they are trying to re-enter civilian
life, just like you, and I'd love to—

MAC: Nope. Sorry, man. I'm done with cameras.

MATTHEW: Perry—

PERRY: Okay. No problem. No problem. Well. Oh, Matthew, I borrowed this too while you were gone.

MATTHEW: Okay.

PERRY: We had a cold spell, so…I don't have heat. I hope you don't mind.

MATTHEW: No.

(He hands him the blanket.)

PERRY: I have a couple other things to return. I didn't think you'd mind.

MATTHEW: I don't.

PERRY: I just didn't want you to think they were stolen or anything.

MATTHEW: Okay. No problem.

PERRY: I'm not a thief.
(He laughs.)

MATTHEW: Okay.

PERRY: Anyway…Nice to meet you Sergeant Johnson. Let me know if you change your mind.

MAC: I won't, but thanks.

PERRY: I live next door just in case you do—

MAC: Nope.

PERRY: Maybe I can stop by tomorrow and just talk to you.

(Silence)

(MAC just looks at PERRY.)

PERRY: Elizabeth, nice to see you again. Matthew never talks about his family. It's nice to see you in the flesh. I'm sure Matthew is happy to have the time with you.

LIZZIE: No. I think he'd rather not.

PERRY: Well. Matthew, looking forward to catching up.

MATTHEW: Got it.

(PERRY *waits, then exits.*)

MATTHEW: Sorry, Mac. Perry's just, just—

MAC: I get it. He's hungry. I just don't do photos anymore. Fool me once, right?

LIZZIE: *(To* MAC*)* You must be some kind of hero.

MAC: I hate that word.

LIZZIE: What did you do?

MATTHEW: If you had watched the documentary, you'd know—

MAC: Can we open a window in here? Something. I feel like I'm in a fucking cave.

Scene 5

(*Slide:* MAC*'s dirt-covered face inside his helmet in Afghanistan.*)

(*Night*)

LIZZIE: Matthew?

(*Silence*)

MATTHEW: What?

LIZZIE: The light?

MATTHEW: What about it?

LIZZIE: Mac, is it too dark in here?

MAC: A little. For my tastes.

(MATTHEW *turns the light on.*)

MATTHEW: How can you sleep with the light on?

LIZZIE: How can you sleep in this abyss?

MATTHEW: Because I'm exhausted. You are exhausting.

LIZZIE: Mac and I aren't used to your crypt. We're living human beings.

MATTHEW: You can't keep doing this, Lizzie.

LIZZIE: I'm a night owl. I can't help it.

MATTHEW: Yes you can.

LIZZIE: How about some music? That's relaxing.

MATTHEW: No.

LIZZIE: Mac?

MAC: I don't mind.

MATTHEW: I was dead asleep.

LIZZIE: Well, we weren't, so it's two against one.
(She gets up.)

(MAC watches LIZZIE move in her nightgown.)

(She looks through the mess that is MATTHEW's C D collection, and stereo.)

LIZZIE: Let's see what you have over here. To put us to sleep.
(She searches.)
I used to put Sarah to sleep with music every night, when she was a baby. My sweet little girl.
(She searches.)
She was so easy then. Everything was so simple.
(She searches.)
Everything made sense. She needed me. I took care of her. I felt useful.

MATTHEW: Uh huh.

(LIZZIE continues to look through music.)

LIZZIE: Pretty pathetic music selection, Matthew.
Shows your age.

(She finds a C D.)

But. Yes. This is good. This is a blast from the past. I
gave this to you…I used to play this for Sarah. I'd tuck
her in and we'd sing together.

(LIZZIE puts a C D in MATTHEW's C D player.)

MATTHEW: *(Groaning)* No. C'mon.

(LIZZIE begins to sing with music.)

(MAC joins in the singing…)

*(MATTHEW slowly gets out of bed. LIZZIE and MAC sing to
him.)*

(MATTHEW turns off the music.)

LIZZIE: Hey.

MAC: I was just getting going, man.

MATTHEW: Go to sleep. Both of you. I don't have time
for this.

LIZZIE: But—

MATTHEW: I really need some rest, Lizzie. I told you.
I'm exhausted.

LIZZIE: But that was so nice. So sweet, that song. Right,
Mac?

MAC: I love that album.

(MATTHEW looks at MAC.)

MAC: What, man? I like musicals.

MATTHEW: This isn't a fucking slumber party. Good
night.

(MATTHEW turns the light off.)

LIZZIE: It's too dark.

(MATTHEW turns the light back on.)

MATTHEW: (Jesus Christ)

MAC: (Superstar.)

(LIZZIE *laughs.*)

MATTHEW: Go to sleep.
(*He returns to his spot on the floor, and turns toward the wall.*)
I mean it.

(MAC *looks at* LIZZIE *and smiles. She smiles back. And stays on the couch next to him.*)

LIZZIE & MAC: (*Singing together very softly*)
Close your eyes, close your eyes…and relax…

Scene 6

(*Slides: Men dead on the battlefield in Afghanistan. A bloody face of a child. The beautiful Afghan woman [same woman as before], praying at sunrise.*)

(*Night*)

(MATTHEW *is on his cellphone, outside.*)

MATTHEW: Well, do you know where they took her?

Scene 7

(*Slide: The beautiful Afghani woman, her scarf falling, smiling at the camera.*)

(*Late morning. There's empty plates of food scattered around.*)

(MATTHEW *is showing* JOHN *and* PERRY *his photos on his computer screen.*)

(LIZZIE *begins to clean up.*)

LIZZIE: Don't you boys have places to be? Or do you just sit at my brother's feet all day?

MATTHEW: They aren't—

PERRY: Hey tell us about Kunar, Sergeant.

MAC: No.

PERRY: C'mon. Tell us about—

MAC: No, man.

LIZZIE: What?

PERRY: Tell them, Matthew.

JOHN: Shut up, Perry.

PERRY: C'mon man. Tell them about it. It's awesome. Tell them about this guy here.

(PERRY *touches* MAC's *shoulder.* MAC *looks at him.*)

MAC: Don't touch me.

(PERRY *takes his hand away.*)

MATTHEW: You really want to hear it again?

PERRY: Yes. C'mon.

LIZZIE: Hear what?

PERRY: Tell your sister, man.

MATTHEW: You've heard it before.

PERRY: So? She hasn't. It's heroic, man. It never gets old.

LIZZIE: What? For Christ's sake.

(JOHN *films.*)

(*The slides on the screen change to the video that* JOHN *Films through the video camera. Sometimes he shoots* LIZZIE *listening or* MATTHEW *speaking, but mostly he shoots* MAC *when* MAC *isn't aware and* MAC's *blank reaction to* MATTHEW's *telling of the story.*)

MATTHEW: Well. We're in the middle of this intense fight in the middle of no where. Fucking Taliban everywhere. I mean everywhere. From all sides. Right, Mac?

(*Silence*)

Right?

(*Silence*)

MAC: Sure.

MATTHEW: And Mac is the only one standing. Literally. I'm laying on the ground, with the camera, trying to keep him in the frame, trying to stay covered, and keep him in the frame the whole time…I'm panicked I'm going to miss something, you know?

PERRY: Yeah. Yeah.

(*To* LIZZIE)

The footage is stunning.

MATTHEW: And it wasn't easy…men have fallen on all sides of us…two are crying and Briggs is yelling for help—

LIZZIE: Who's Briggs?

PERRY: Mac's best friend.

LIZZIE: Why didn't you help him?

MATTHEW: What was I saying?

PERRY: "Briggs is yelling for help."

MATTHEW: Yeah, yeah. Right. Briggs is yelling for help, and Mac is trying to get over to him, but the bullets keeps coming as he's trying to fire back as he's trying as hard as he can to get to Briggs. I mean, he's in the middle of it, fighting for his life, and Briggs is dying over there. Bleeding out. It's a mess. And Mac is amazing. He's superman. A warrior in the throws of battle. Mythic.

PERRY: He looks like a movie star, seriously—

MATTHEW: I'd never seen anything like it. Every muscle alert, every cell on task, every ounce of him focused, ready. Superhuman. Incredible. Right?

(Silence)

MAC: If you say so.
(To JOHN*)*
You better not be shooting me with that thing.

JOHN: I'm not. It's cool.

MATTHEW: And I'm still just trying to keep Mac in the fucking frame, while not getting killed myself. I mean, I'm—
(He leans over on the couch, pantomiming the struggle to keep the camera on MAC.*)*
I'm on my side like this, just trying to keep it all in the frame and Mac looks almost, almost, fucking otherworldly, the whole thing is lit with this weird perfect light—

PERRY: Perfect—

LIZZIE: So why didn't you just help him?

MATTHEW: What?

LIZZIE: Why didn't you just put the camera down and help him?

MATTHEW: I'm not trained to do that.

LIZZIE: Still.

MATTHEW: Still what?

LIZZIE: Seems you might have helped.

MATTHEW: No. I couldn't. That's not my job.

LIZZIE: This was supposed to be about me.

MATTHEW: What?

LIZZIE: *This.*

MATTHEW: What are you talking about?

LIZZIE: John was supposed to be filming me. My story. "The Heroin Housewife." Isn't that what you called it, John?

JOHN: Well, well…this, this is part of your life too, Elizabeth. And I haven't really settled on a title—

LIZZIE: How?

JOHN: How what?

LIZZIE: How's this part of my life?

JOHN: He's your brother.

LIZZIE: This has nothing to do with me. At all.

JOHN: It's interesting.

LIZZIE: But it's not about me. My life. Why film it?

MATTHEW: All this is already in my documentary anyway. He can't use it.

JOHN: Well maybe. You never know. Perry, could you get out of my way?

PERRY: I'm not in your way.

JOHN: Yes you are. Move.

LIZZIE: You're hogging the spotlight, Matthew.

MATTHEW: We're just reminiscing. Right Mac? These guys were interested, so—

LIZZIE: You're bragging. In front of your friends. That's all I've seen you do—

MATTHEW: I'm not bragging. It's what happened. You wanted to know—

PERRY: He's not bragging. He's won a lot of awards.

JOHN: I consider it part of your story, Elizabeth. Background. Family. I could, maybe I could use some of it— You're in my way, Perry.

PERRY: How?

LIZZIE: Let them rent his damn documentary again if they want to hear it. Right, Mac? You really want to sit around and listen to this?

MAC: Nope.

LIZZIE: See?

MATTHEW: You saved Briggs that day. You saved his fucking life.

MAC: I did my job.

MATTHEW: You did more than—

LIZZIE: It must be upsetting.

PERRY: You got a medal.

MAC: So.

PERRY: I don't think most people realize what you guys have gone through over there.

MATTHEW: That's why I was trying to keep him in the frame!

MAC: I don't need to talk about it every fucking day.

MATTHEW: Shouldn't this country see what has been sacrificed for their "freedom"—

PERRY: Exactly—

JOHN: Can you just stand over there?

PERRY: Why?

JOHN: Your big head is in my way.

MAC: The country will see what they want to see. I just came here to relax, man. I need a fucking beer. Something.

MATTHEW: But we can't stop showing them the truth.

PERRY: Exactly.

JOHN: Shut up, Perry. Why are you here anyway? No one likes you.

PERRY: Why would you say something like that?

MAC: I never signed on to be your poster boy for "truth".

MATTHEW: Okay.

LIZZIE: I still think *you* could have tried to save that guy Riggs.

MATTHEW: *Br*iggs! *Br*iggs! I wasn't qualified. Damn it, Lizzie. You don't even remember his fucking name.

LIZZIE: You're a person. With two hands. That's all I'm saying.

(JOHN *turns off the camera. Suddenly quiet.* MAC *is starting to get anxious. He stands up.*)

MATTHEW: I'm not a fucking medic.

LIZZIE: Neither is Mac.

MATTHEW: He has a gun. That's his job. You have no idea what you're talking about—

LIZZIE: Just seems like common decency. Who wants more coffee?

MAC: Me. Please. I need something.

MATTHEW: You've never been to war. You wouldn't understand.

PERRY: You really don't know what it's like until you're there.

LIZZIE: So I can't have an opinion?

MATTHEW/PERRY: No.

LIZZIE: Okay. You're the expert, Matthew. You and your friends, playing soldiers. Getting off on it, with your cameras.

MATTHEW: Okay. That's enough.

LIZZIE: I'm making more coffee. I need to get jacked up. It's all I've got.

(MAC *follows* LIZZIE *to the kitchen area.*)

LIZZIE: John, you want to come film me making coffee?
(Silence)
John?

JOHN: I'm, I'm kinda taking a break at the moment.

LIZZIE: My whole life has been built around this activity. Pretty interesting stuff. I'll give you lots of juicy, sordid details about how I used to plan my day.

JOHN: Oh. Okay.
(He gets up to follow her.)

(In the corner of the kitchen area, MAC takes out a pill bottle and fishes and out pill. LIZZIE steps beside him.)

(LIZZIE and MAC talk in one side of the stage, while PERRY, JOHN, and MATTHEW remain on the other side. The conversations move quickly, overlapping.)

PERRY: Did you tell Matthew you didn't go to Somalia?

JOHN: Thanks, dickhead.

MATTHEW: What?

LIZZIE: You alright?

PERRY: He didn't go. I did.

MAC: Sure.

MATTHEW: Why?

LIZZIE: What's that?

JOHN: It just—

MAC: Just something for my head.

JOHN: Just wasn't the right project for me.

PERRY: They told me you couldn't do it.

LIZZIE: Can I see?
(She holds out her hand.)

PERRY: You freaked out.

JOHN: Bullshit.

MAC: You're trying to stay clean.

MATTHEW: What happened?

LIZZIE: I just want to look at it.

JOHN: Perry took my fucking job.

PERRY: I did not.

MATTHEW: *(To* MAC *and* LIZZIE*)* What are you guys doing?

MAC: Your brother would kill me.

PERRY: You freaked out. You got scared.

MATTHEW: Mac? Lizzie?

LIZZIE: Who made him captain of the ship?

JOHN: No.

PERRY: So they called me.

JOHN: You're like a sand shark—

LIZZIE: Please—

JOHN: Eating everything in its path.

LIZZIE: Just let me hold the pill.

PERRY: No I'm not——

JOHN: I know who you are!

LIZZIE: Whatever it is—

MATTHEW: What the fuck's your problem, John?

LIZZIE: It's a good test for me.

MATTHEW: We're your friends.

JOHN: Please.

MAC: It's just Xanax.

LIZZIE: Xanax?

JOHN: The friend you never call or write. You'd throw any "friend" under the bus—

LIZZIE: That's all they give you?

JOHN: Both of you—

MAC: Who?

MATTHEW: I've been busy—

LIZZIE: The government.

MAC: No—

MATTHEW: I have a lot of shit in my life right now—
(To LIZZIE *and* MAC*)*
What are you guys talking about?

JOHN: And Perry? You didn't even talk to me before you took my place —

PERRY: There wasn't time—

MAC: I've gotten other things—

JOHN: To make one phone call? To walk upstairs?

LIZZIE: Like what?

JOHN: You're both great friends.

MAC: Zoloft—

PERRY: Did you want to have a conversation?

LIZZIE: Of course—

PERRY: You've been drunk for weeks -

LIZZIE: Prozac? Paxil?

JOHN: I bet you love me like this. Right, Matthew?

MAC: Tried them.

MATTHEW: How? What?

JOHN: This.

MAC: That shit made me feel dead.

MATTHEW: Look, John, you want help, I'm here -

LIZZIE: Depakote?

MAC: Tried that too—

MATTHEW: But I don't need your bullshit right now. Okay?

MAC: But not for me.

JOHN: Some friend.

LIZZIE: Ativan?

JOHN: You don't care about me.

MAC: I ran out.

MATTHEW: Yes we do.

LIZZIE: Uh-huh.

PERRY: You need help.

LIZZIE: Klonopin?

JOHN: Shut up.

MAC: Had that too. Liked that.

JOHN: I'm sure you guys just love to see me me fucked up and —

PERRY: Why?

JOHN: And, and—

PERRY: Why would we enjoy that?

JOHN: I'm talented. You're jealous. More work for you.

MATTHEW: Jesus, John—

LIZZIE: Remeron?

PERRY: I don't want more work.

JOHN: Don't lie, Perry.

MAC: No. But some painkillers.

JOHN: God!

LIZZIE: What kind?

(JOHN *trips.*)

JOHN: I used to be just like you, Matthew.

MATTHEW: Give me your coffee.

MAC: Oxycodone. For my back.

JOHN: Remember?

LIZZIE: Ah yes.

MATTHEW: Your coffee!

JOHN: I was better than you, Perry.

LIZZIE: Perfect.

MATTHEW: Give me your coffee—

JOHN: No—

LIZZIE: Now we're talking, Mac.

JOHN: I was more like Matthew.

LIZZIE: Let me see.

MAC: No.

MATTHEW: I told you not to bring booze in here—

JOHN: And now I—

LIZZIE: Please?

MAC: No.

JOHN: I just don't see the point.

PERRY: You're not better than me.

JOHN: I used to be just like Matthew. I'd risk anything for a picture of a bloody face. It was all I cared about.

PERRY: People change—

JOHN: I will punch you.
(*To* MATTHEW)
Remember when I was like you?

MATTHEW: Stop saying that, you fuck. You're nothing like me. Give me your coffee.
(He finally grabs JOHN's *coffee and smells it.)*
Damn it. I told you not to bring booze in here. I specifically said, no fucking booze, in my house.
(To LIZZIE*)*
Lizzie!

LIZZIE: Give me the painkiller, Mac.

JOHN: I don't know what happened.

MATTHEW: Coffee, Lizzie!

LIZZIE: *(To* MAC*)* Please?

MAC: I can't.

JOHN: I just don't see the point anymore.

LIZZIE: Just let me hold it.

MATTHEW: *(To* LIZZIE*)* Coffee!

JOHN: How do you do it?

MAC: No.

JOHN: Matthew?

MATTHEW: Stop it.

JOHN: Tell me. Seriously. I need to know.

LIZZIE: I'll just hold it for comfort.

PERRY: You just need a break.

JOHN: Shut up!

MATTHEW: Lizzie, where's the damn coffee?

LIZZIE: What, Matthew? What?

MATTHEW: John needs the coffee.

LIZZIE: I'm waiting for him to film it.

MATTHEW: What? Why?

LIZZIE: It's part of my life story.

MATTHEW: Just make the damn coffee!

LIZZIE: My yet to be discovered oeuvre.

MATTHEW: No one cares!

LIZZIE: I care.
(To MAC)
Just give me the painkiller, please?

MATTHEW: Why are you whispering?

LIZZIE: I was just asking Mac why he thought you didn't save his friend.

MATTHEW: Fuck you!
(He throws JOHN's *coffee mug across the room.)*
FUCK YOU! YOU JUNKIE PIECE OF SHIT!
*(*JOHN *films.)*
(The screen captures a close up image of LIZZIE's *face.)*

MATTHEW: You've never done one fucking thing to help another person. Not one. You want someone to film you making coffee?! Fuck you! Go home!

(Silence)

LIZZIE: I raised a child

MATTHEW: And left her for smack—

MATTHEW: When you put yourself out in the middle of some real struggle, and suffering—

LIZZIE: Matthew—

MATTHEW: Some real conflict, and try and capture it for the rest of world to see, to understand, to *witness*, then you can ask me why I didn't put down my camera.

LIZZIE: I'm asking you now.

MATTHEW: I was doing my job. Something you have no concept of. *Work.* Responsibility. You piece of shit.

*(*MAC *grabs* LIZZIE's *hand and slips her a pill.)*

LIZZIE: And it's that important? Sacrificing a man's life for a good photo?

MATTHEW: You have no idea what I've sacrificed.

LIZZIE: What do you think Mac?

MATTHEW: Tell her.
(*Silence*)
Was it my job that day to save Briggs?

MAC: Matthew wasn't in Afghanistan to be in the Army.

MATTHEW: See? Fuck you, Lizzie.

MAC: He was there to make a movie.

MATTHEW: You agreed to it! It was my job! You wanted to do it!

MAC: I know—

MATTHEW: So what's your problem?

MAC: Look man, I've got no problem with you.

MATTHEW: Good—

MAC: But it didn't do anything, that film. But make me look foolish.

MATTHEW: You didn't look foolish.
(*Silence*)
You didn't look foolish, Mac. I promise—

MAC: Did it end the war?

MATTHEW: Did you think it would?

MAC: You told me it might. It could. "If people see how awful it is here, Mac, if people really see how futile this fight is, we might really change something. We could change things for everyone here, man. You can help me do that."

MATTHEW: I still believe that.

MAC: Change what?

MATTHEW: Well, people, if people—

MAC: Briggs survived, sure, but he's half gone, and I lost fifteen good friends and there are more over there and nothing has changed. Except now a lot of people have seen me cry on T V and think they know what it feels like to be me, and think they know something about war.

MATTHEW: Mac—

MAC: They don't know shit. And worse, they don't care.

MATTHEW: You don't know that.

MAC: See what I learned from that movie, Matthew, what I really understood when I watched it, like a fucking light bulb man, is that we're both nothing but tools for this government. They got us both.

MATTHEW: No. Not me—

MAC: Oh, you thought it was just me? I'm the tool. You were going to prove that I'm nothing but cannon fodder?

MATTHEW: No, I didn't say that. Don't put words in my—

MAC: Why do you think they let you come live with us, eat with us, film us, become buddies? So people will know the "truth"?

MATTHEW: Yes. It's our job. To be objective—

PERRY: That's right—

MAC: No. I figured it out, man. No.

MATTHEW: Yes. Our job is to—

MAC: You help the government make sure that the people love us, cry with us, send us care packages, worry about our P T S D, maybe want to fuck us when

we come home *(if we're lucky)*, and see only what the
government decides they should see, so they can just
keep spending their dollars, and we can keep going
back. Or die. Or kill ourselves. Whatever fucking
comes first.

MATTHEW: No.

MAC: What do you think *embedded* means, man? It's
rigged.

MATTHEW/PERRY: No.

MAC: We're all sucking on the same fucked-up tit.
Right? We go back over there the minute we can, even
if we hate it. They got us hooked.

MATTHEW: No—

PERRY: Not true—

MAC: How many times have you been over there? Five,
six, seven? And Iraq? And where else did you tell me
you went...Libya? Gaza? And, and where you going
next? Syria? Back to Iraq? Bet you can't wait—

MATTHEW: It's my job—

PERRY: Yeah—

MAC: And most of the pictures you shoot, the really
serious fucked-up shit, no one will ever see. You told
me that.

MATTHEW: There are rules—

PERRY: Yeah—

MAC: It's rigged.

LIZZIE: I don't think it's worth it.

MATTHEW: You don't even know what I fucking shoot!
You won't even watch the films I send you. What do
you care? Jesus Christ. Shut up or get out!

LIZZIE: I know every picture you've had published. I look for your name every day. I can't imagine carrying those violent images in my mind—

MATTHEW: Jesus, Lizzie. Shut up. Shut up.

LIZZIE: I think John's the only one with some common sense to just stay home and get drunk. Get out. Right, John?

(JOHN *is staring at his camera, while it films his foot.*)

JOHN: What? I'm sorry. I wasn't really listening.
(To PERRY*)*
What was the question?

PERRY: It doesn't matter.

JOHN: Shut up.

MATTHEW: You don't know anything about me, Lizzie. So let's just stop this right now. Go home. All of you. I'm done.

JOHN: What was the damn question? What are you talking about?

PERRY: It's not important. Forget it, man.

JOHN: You forget it. Asshole.

LIZZIE: I know a lot about you by the photos you shoot, Matthew.

MATTHEW: No you don't. Get out.

LIZZIE: Don't you see beauty anywhere? Why can't you shoot beautiful things? Like birds. Or flowers. Happy people. *Life.*

MATTHEW: Please.

LIZZIE: Why focus on war? On death? On suffering? What's wrong with you? There are so many other things—

MATTHEW: Because it exists.

LIZZIE: Life exists too. Don't you see beauty anymore? Anywhere?

MATTHEW: What do you care?

LIZZIE: You're my brother. I love you. I want you to be—

MATTHEW: So?

LIZZIE: I want you to be happy.

MATTHEW: Since when?

LIZZIE: Matthew—

MATTHEW: *Happy*? Do you even know what that means? You're going to talk to me about happiness, about beauty, with your fucking heroin habit, and, and bullshit life—

LIZZIE: At least I know what love feels like. That has made me happy. You've never even loved—

MATTHEW: Oh, you want to see pictures of love? Really? You want to see love? Is that what you think is important? Pictures of love?
(He goes to his stack of photos and throws photos of an Afghani woman at LIZZIE.*)*
Here.
(He throws more in the room.)
Here. Here. Here.
(He covers the room in pictures of a beautiful Afghani woman.)
You think you know me now?

*(*MAC *picks up one of the photos.* JOHN *and* PERRY *also pick them up.)*

MATTHEW: You think that's not suffering?

*(*LIZZIE *picks up one of the photos.)*

MATTHEW: Let me tell you something. Love is just as painful. It's worse.

MAC: You're in love with her?

MATTHEW: Coming home was a mistake.
(He starts looking for his shoes.)
Where are my shoes?
(He starts tearing through stuff.)
Where are my fucking shoes? I try and do the right
thing, do something for you Lizzie, when you need me,
and all you do is shit on me, my life, my fucking *career*.
Why? Why? Because you love me? Fuck you. I'm a
good guy. You know that? I'm one of the good ones!
I try and do my part. I try and do the right thing. Do
you know what that is? To care about anyone else but
yourself? You don't know shit about love.

LIZZIE: That's not true—

MATTHEW: Ask your daughter.

(Silence)

LIZZIE: That's not fair. You have no idea—

MATTHEW: Fuck fair! Nothing is fair!
(Silence)
And I may fail, Mac, but I try. I'm no fucking tool. For
anybody. No one. You hear me?

MAC: You're in love with her—

MATTHEW: Who takes care of <u>me</u> when I need help?
When I fuck up? If I ruin everything?—

PERRY: *(I would—)*

MATTHEW: Huh? *Fair*?! You think you would come
to my rescue, Lizzie? Drop everything? Clear your
schedule? Spend two days on a plane? Open up your
home? Just for me?
(Silence)
That's what I thought. I have no where to go to get any
kind of rest or relief. Or *simple* fucking love.
(He finds his shoes under JOHN's *camera.)*

Have you been recording this?

JOHN: I don't know.

MATTHEW: What do you mean, you don't know?

(MATTHEW *kicks* JOHN, *hard.*)

JOHN: Hey.

MATTHEW: Get the fuck out of my face.

JOHN: I might have left it on. At some point.

(MATTHEW *reaches for the camera.* JOHN *takes it back.*)

JOHN: I'm sure you'd love to get hands on all of this and take it away from me. Take away all my work and, and stories and talent. I was like you, remember.

(MATTHEW *shoves* JOHN, *camera in hand.*)

MATTHEW: You have never been like me. Alright? You're weak, selfish and pathetic.

JOHN: Maybe.

(MATTHEW *grabs the camera from* JOHN.)

JOHN: Give it back.

MATTHEW: Fuck you.

PERRY: You need help, John—

JOHN: Oh fuck you, Perry. Please. You make me want to vomit, you fucking phony. You didn't even come to the funeral of two of your best friends.

PERRY: Maybe I wasn't ready—

JOHN: I want you to bring back everything you've ever borrowed from me. Right now.

(MAC *takes another pill.*)

PERRY: I didn't want that fucking Somalia job. I hated every minute of it. I would have left if I could. I was miserable. Does that make you happy?

JOHN: Yes. Actually. It does.

(PERRY *exits.*)

MAC: You're in love with her?

(JOHN *is trying to get his camera from* MATTHEW.)

MATTHEW: Knock it off, John!

JOHN: It's mine.

MATTHEW: I will kick you in the face if you don't let go.

(ALLEN LIGHTHOUSE *enters through the open door. He's mid-fifties. Well-groomed. He wears a beautiful, expensive suit.*)

ALLEN: That, outside, is hell. It's a hundred degrees and I have to walk through mouth-breathers from Missouri. Give me a fucking break. Where's Matthew? Is this Matthew Milton's apartment.

(LIZZIE *just looks at* ALLEN.)

ALLEN: That front door is wide open downstairs. Why are there no locks? This is New York, for Christ's sake. Are you crazy? What's going on here?

(MATTHEW *and* JOHN *are still wrestling for the camera.*)

MATTHEW: Dammit, John!

ALLEN: Lizard, pack your things.

LIZZIE: You're early.

ALLEN: Well, I thought about it and realized I may have been unfair. I'm sorry.

LIZZIE: Uh huh.

ALLEN: So. We're ready to see you. Pack your things and come home.

LIZZIE: No.

(ALLEN *grabs his head.*)

ALLEN: Matthew, do you have any scotch? I take one look at your sister, and I need a drink. And all those goddamn tourists out there, I wanted to wring their necks.

(JOHN *finally lets go, let's* MATTHEW *have his camera.*)

JOHN: Fine. Fuck you.

ALLEN: What the hell? What's going on here?

MAC: Matthew?

(MATTHEW *rests on the couch. Suddenly exhausted*)

MATTHEW: Can you all leave. Now.

ALLEN: What is this?

MATTHEW: Take her, Allen.

JOHN: I need a drink.

LIZZIE: I don't want to go—

ALLEN: Lizard. Now. Please.
(*He gets close to* LIZZIE, *tries to put his arms around her.*)
Please. Please don't make a scene. We've had enough of those, haven't we? Sarah and I miss you. I'm admitting that I was wrong. I shouldn't have—

LIZZIE: You stink.

ALLEN: No. Now. Don't start that—

LIZZIE: I can smell the house on you.

ALLEN: Don't start with that. Please. Our house is—

LIZZIE: It's awful. Get away.

ALLEN: Lizard. For God's sake.

LIZZIE: Get away.

MAC: Matthew. Did you talk to her?

ALLEN: I don't stink!

JOHN: Who wants a drink?

ALLEN: Me.

MAC: Does she forgive me?

(Silence)
I had to do it. Did you tell her that?

MATTHEW: Yes.

MAC: It was my job. Did you tell her that?

MATTHEW: Mac. Please.

MAC: Did you tell her that! Your fucking girlfriend!

MATTHEW: It was her brother.

ALLEN: Lizard—

MAC: I didn't know who he was! He had a gun! Why was he carrying a gun? He was Taliban—

MATTHEW: It was Briggs gun. He found it—

ALLEN: Let's go—

MAC: How was I supposed to know that?! He was pointing it at me! At you! Did you tell her that?!

MATTHEW: He was a kid.

(PERRY enters and throws camera equipment at John: Lenses, a bag, a flash, socks, candles, a pillow, a couple of shirts, some shampoo, a back scratcher. Then exits just as quickly as he left.)

ALLEN: I don't know what the hell is going on here, but I need a goddamn drink. This is ridiculous.

JOHN: I have scotch—

ALLEN: Scotch—

JOHN: I have beer, I have…oh, let me think.

ALLEN: Scotch. If you don't you mind. I'll pay you for it.

MAC: What else you got?

JOHN: What are you looking for?

MAC: Anything, man. Anything. I need something. Now—

JOHN: I've got quite a few other type things.

MAC: Can I come with you?

JOHN: Be my guest.

MATTHEW: Mac.

MAC: Fuck you.

(JOHN and MAC exit.)

(LIZZIE stands looking at MATTHEW.)

(ALLEN finds himself stepping on photos.)

ALLEN: Jesus Christ. These are yours, Matthew? On the floor? How do you live like this?
(He picks up the camera and looks through the lens, turns it toward LIZZIE.)
I wanted to be a photographer when I was a boy, but my father wouldn't let me. He felt it was small, selfish pursuit, so…I went into banking. Look how that turned out.

(On screen. Video of LIZZIE's face. She turns and looks directly at the camera.)

ALLEN: One minute you're going about your life, thinking you are doing what's best for your family; your child, your wife, you're thinking you'd do anything to make them happy…anything…and the next minute you're following a police officer into a dark building, up to a filthy room on the fifth floor, looking for the beautiful woman you married and hoping you won't find her asleep in the arms of gaunt heroin addict, again…but you do…so you pull her from him, block out the shouting…and carry her home…that's your new life, carrying your wife home… and everything that came before that minute has been strangled.

LIZZIE: Because it has. It's gone.

(ALLEN *puts down the camera.*)

ALLEN: You have everything any human being could possibly want.

LIZZIE: I never wanted everything. I just wanted something *interesting*.

ALLEN: What's the difference?

LIZZIE: Oh Allen.

ALLEN: What?

LIZZIE: Go home.

ALLEN: Lizard.

(LIZZIE *goes and gets on her knees next to* MATTHEW.)

LIZZIE: Who's that woman?
(Silence)
How does Mac know who—

MATTHEW: He killed her brother.

(Silence)

LIZZIE: And you—

MATTHEW: I was doing a story about her. And… And I fucked up.

LIZZIE: How?

MATTHEW: Her parents married her off. Somewhere.

LIZZIE: Well, you can—

MATTHEW: No. You don't understand. I fucked it up.

LIZZIE: How?

MATTHEW: I touched her.

LIZZIE: So?

MATTHEW: I touched her face. I touched her hand. I touched—

LIZZIE: But—

MATTHEW: I wasn't supposed to touch her.

LIZZIE: Why not?

MATTHEW: I wasn't supposed to touch her! Jesus! What part don't you get?

ALLEN: Lizard. Please. Enough is enough. Pack your things.

LIZZIE: I'm not going.

ALLEN: Yes you are, now—

LIZZIE: No.

MATTHEW: You're not staying here.

LIZZIE: What? No. Matthew—

MATTHEW: You've worn out your welcome, Lizzie.

LIZZIE: But—

MATTHEW: I'm serious. I'm done. I can't—

LIZZIE: I know you think I'm nothing but a piece of shit junkie, but I'm also your sister and I love you. I love very much. We're all that's left of our family. We're it. And believe it or not, your opinion of me matters. It matters a lot. More than you know. I used to worship you.
(She shows him the pill in her hand.)
I have held this pain pill and didn't take it.

MATTHEW: Where'd you get it?

ALLEN: What's that?

LIZZIE: I didn't take it. I'm clean now.

(LIZZIE hands the pill to MATTHEW.)

LIZZIE: I'm clean. See?

(MATTHEW looks at the pill, then swallows it.)

(JOHN and MAC enter with the scotch. They are drunk and stoned.)

JOHN: Scotch! Who wants it?

ALLEN: Me.

JOHN: Elizabeth. Let me tell you something.

(LIZZIE *takes a seat beside* MATTHEW *on the couch.*)

(JOHN *hands* ALLEN *the scotch.* ALLEN *drinks from the bottle.*)

JOHN: Elizabeth. Listen. Listen. I think you and I, have something very special. I do. And I really shouldn't be doing this, Elizabeth. Falling in love. I could influence the story. Change the narrative. Lose myself…I really should keep a distance. It's healthier…I think I've got some good stuff. I do. But I think we can go deeper. I think there's lots of dark stuff you haven't shared on camera yet. People really want secrets. That's what everyone's really waiting for—
(*He falls, then sits on the floor.*)
Wow. It's really quite comfortable here. The floor is more comfortable than most people think.

MAC: Hey, man. What are you doing down there?

JOHN: Enjoying the floor.

MAC: What are you enjoying about it?

JOHN: That it exists. It's here for me right now. Thanks, floor.

(MAC *picks up the camera and turns it on* JOHN.)

(*On the screen: video:* JOHN *smiles for the camera.*)

JOHN: I should have shaved, huh? Don't make me look like I have a double chin. I hate that.

(MAC *turns the camera on* MATTHEW.)

(MATTHEW *sits on the couch, staring at the floor.*)

(ALLEN *drinks and drinks.*)

ALLEN: Lizard. Get your things. Right now. It's not a question any more. It's an order.

LIZZIE: Who do you think you are?

ALLEN: Your husband.

LIZZIE: I'll come home when I'm ready.

(On the screen. Video: MATTHEW's face as he stares at the floor. At all the photos)

ALLEN: What about Sarah. I promised her you'd be coming home today—

LIZZIE: She can wait a few more days.

ALLEN: She's your daughter.

LIZZIE: I want to stay with my brother.

ALLEN: What about me?

LIZZIE: What about you?

(ALLEN throws the bottle against the wall.)

(Stunned, everyone looks at ALLEN.)

MAC: Shit, man. Watch it.

JOHN: That was expensive.

ALLEN: Why do you have to torture me? No matter what you do, it's meant to hurt me. You know that?

LIZZIE: I'm sorry.

(JOHN curls up on his side.)

JOHN: I have more booze upstairs. I have more. Right, floor?

(ALLEN gathers himself.)

ALLEN: What will I tell Sarah?

LIZZIE: Tell her I'm with Uncle Matthew and it's very important and if she wants to come visit him, she is welcome.

ALLEN: I'm not letting her come to this place. Look at it.

LIZZIE: Then Matthew will come visit her. Maybe we'll take a little trip together.

ALLEN: What about me? What about what I want?

LIZZIE: You have a house full of things you want.

(ALLEN stares at LIZZIE.)

LIZZIE: You've got the whole world, Allen.

ALLEN: I want you.

LIZZIE: My brother needs me.

ALLEN: I want you.

LIZZIE: My brother needs me.

(Unsure of what to do next, ALLEN exits.)

(MAC sways, then puts the camera down. He joins JOHN on the floor.)

MAC: This is very comfortable down here.

JOHN: Isn't it?

MAC: Solid.

JOHN: I could stay here forever. I'll take the whole goddamn world right here, on this floor.

(LIZZIE and MATTHEW sit side by side. She puts her hand on his leg.)

(MAC softly hums song from earlier.)

(MATTHEW puts his head in his hands and cries.)

(MAC continues to hum softly.)

(LIZZIE takes a blanket and covers her brother, as he lies down on the couch. She tucks him in. Kisses his cheek. She begins to clean up the apartment, by carefully collecting the photos from the floor, one by one. Lights fade.)

END OF PLAY.

www.ingramcontent.com/pod-product-compliance
Lightning Source LLC
Chambersburg PA
CBHW052202090426
42741CB00010B/2380